THINGKINGS

TALES OF INANIMATE'S EMOTION

ANNAMALAI
SHANMUGANATHAN

Made with ♥ on the Notion Press Platform
www.notionpress.com

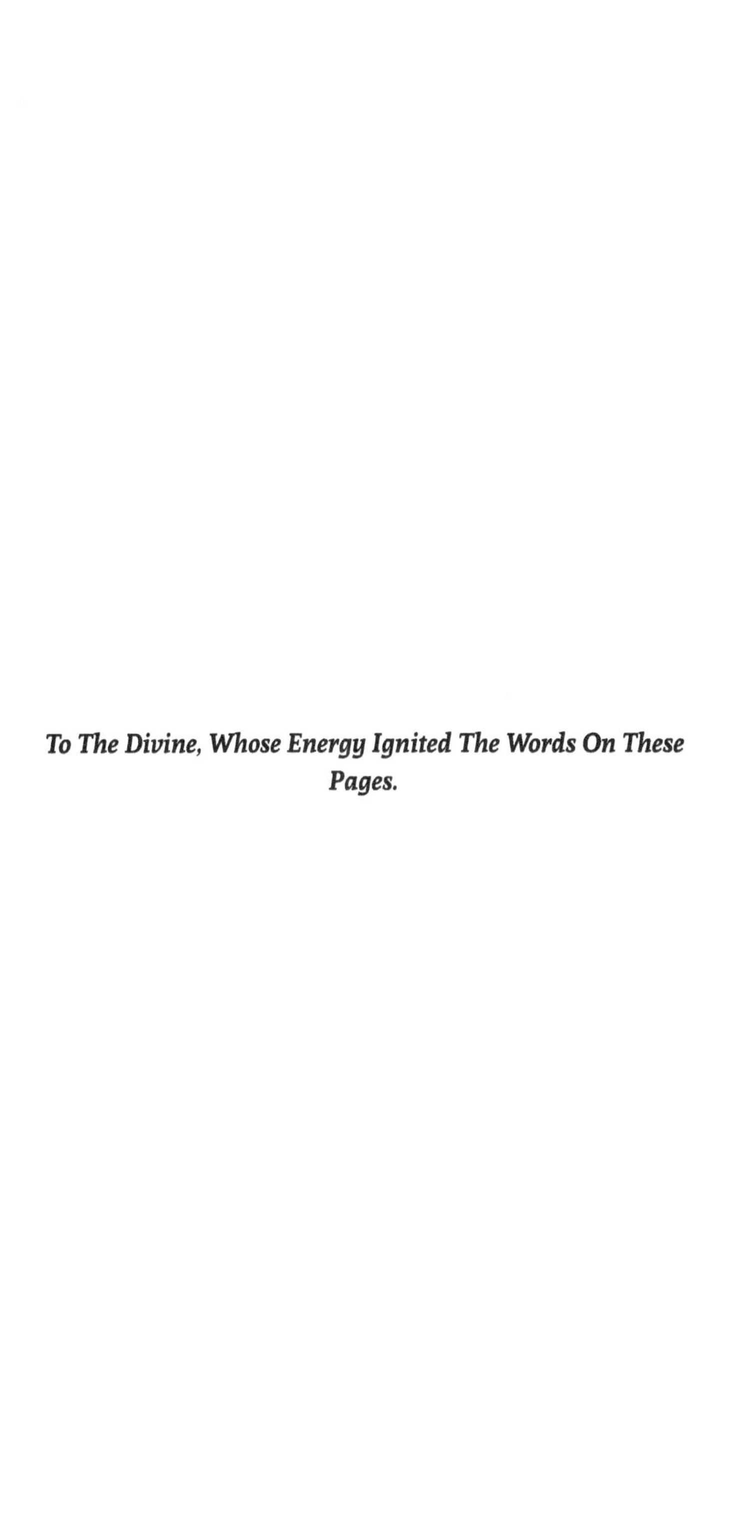

To The Divine, Whose Energy Ignited The Words On These Pages.

Contents

FOREWORD

All Creative inventions in this world are started with a simple Question

WHAT IF?

In a Similar way an Idea cracked in my mind , What If the Inanimates (Non-Living things) have emotions and feelings like human beings?

I had tried to give a word form of this idea and that idea is martertialize into a book of short stories.

I hope you would like this concept and enjoy the stories.

PREFACE

*Instead of a preface, I can say this is a kind of **disclaimer.***

This book is a compilation of standalone short stories.

The stories are not connected to one another.

It is purely fictional work.

If there are any coincidences with anybody, kindly thank my imaginary skills.

There are no instances of smoking or alcohol consumption in this book because I strongly believe both are injurious to mind & body's health.

Acknowledgements

From the Heart:

*Thank you **Ramesh Leela Shankar** My friend, well-wisher, and esteemed writer, I cannot express my gratitude enough. If our paths had not crossed, I doubt I would have ever written a story in English. Your English books have been a profound inspiration, igniting a passion for the language within me. This is my second book and i would like to keep this acknowledgment forever in my book.*

To the Brain:

*Thanks to evolving technologies, I vividly recall writing my first novel in 2003 entirely by hand using a pencil and a school notebook. Unfortunately, due to limited exposure and financial constraints, I couldn't bring it to fruition. After fire and the wheel, the internet is undoubtedly one of the most significant inventions in human history. While it won't physically increase the speed of Earth, it has rev olutionized the way we live, communicate, and access information. I am grateful for **online publishing platforms**, **Google**, and advanced language models like **Gemini,** which have made it possible for authors like me to share our work with a global audience.*

To the Human Being:

*# My colleague - **Shiva Shankara Narayanan** We learn things from everyone. I learn this from you !!!*

*# My Friend - **Christopher Samuel** Thanks Buddy!!! You are my ray of Hope!!!*

*# My Everything - **Alamelu** - Because of you everything is possible!!!*

*# My Readers - **who appreicated, commented, suggested after reading my book.***

Prologue

All I would like to say to everyone is: Love yourself. That is the best way to beautify the life we live among other living and non-living beings..

Even it is an animate or inanimate - Love is the eternal source of Soul

- with love

Annamalai Shanmuganathan

Let us Begin ......

I
DESTINY

Subesh:

It was a sunny day in Chennai. Subesh, an young man, was studying the last semester of his final year in Master of Commerce. His dream was to get a placement in BSRK India Ltd. one of the biggest auditing firm.

He was applying for a trainee post on that company's website. It is important to dream about our futures, but it is even more important to work towards them. Subesh was doing that. After submitting his application, he received an acknowledgment email confirming its receipt.

If we do our part, the universe will help us succeed. He went to college the next day and received an email on his college portal informing him that BSRK India Ltd would be conducting interviews for trainees the following week.

Subesh was excited about the news and began preparing for his interview. He researched BSRK's website, noting details about the company, its revenue, and client base. He also watched YouTube videos on interview skills, focusing on how to speak, behave, and dress appropriately.

Subesh realized the importance of speaking confidently and learned that a light-colored full-sleeve shirt and dark-colored trousers are ideal for interviews. He has a dozen dark-colored trousers, but he doesn't have a light-colored full-sleeve shirt. He decided to buy a new one.

The White Shirt:

In the evening Subesh went to the Ranganathan street, a bustling commercial street located in T. Nagar of Chennai. He found one small ready-made clothing shop. He went inside and asked for a light colored shirts. The shopkeeper inquired about his shirt size and displayed options in light blue, light peach, sandalwood, and light yellow. He opened the packaging of these shirts and offered them to Subesh for trying on.

Subesh tried on the shirts, but none of them fit him perfectly. The blue shirt had slightly longer sleeves, the peach color wasn't flattering, and he didn't like the material of the sandalwood and yellow shirts. Subesh asked for more options but found none. As he was about to leave, he noticed a poster advertising white shirts in the shop. Suddenly, an idea struck him, and he asked the shop owner...

"Anna do you have white shirts" Subesh asked the shopkeeper

"Yes Thambi, you have asked for light colored shirts so i was showing only color shirts? do you need white?" Shopkeeper replied

No body considering white as a color becuase There is no dark white or light white, yes it does not have any shade. This is the reason why all the good things are compared with White. More imortantly as per science White reflects all the light it doesnot absorbs any light.

A red object looks red because it reflects red light and absorbs all other colors. A green object looks green because it reflects green light and absorbs all other colors. A white object looks white because it is made up of all colors combined, and it reflects all of them.

Philosophically, white does not have any desires and does not absorb anything for itself.

Subesh asked for a shirt to try on. The shopkeeper gave him one. He went to the fitting room and put on the shirt.

He looked in the mirror. The shirt fit him perfectly, and he looked good in the white color. White doesn't absorb any color, but Subesh was captivated by this color. At the same time a magic happened , while Subesh was looking in the mirror, the white shirt was also looking itself and subesh in the mirror.

The white shirt looked and felt very good on Subesh.

It began speaking to itself, "Today I am feeling free. Until now, these people have packed me inside plastic. How terrible it is! How do these humans live with it? God knows."

Subesh felt very light and good in this shirt. This was because of the white shirt's happiness. It began to reflect its maximum level. Subesh felt himself looking very good in this shirt. More than that, the white shirt felt very good when Subesh wore it. The white shirt performed very well like an interview. It looks very good in terms of color and comfort. Subesh was impressed and decided to buy it.

The white shirt passed its interview. Subesh purchased it from the shop owner. The shop owner packed the shirt back in the plastic cover and gave it to Subesh. This time, it didn't feel bad inside the plastic because it knew its destiny.

White also absorbs, perhaps not physically, but emotionally.

The interview day, Subesh wore the white shirt. No, the white shirt was worn by Subesh. When Subesh was wearing the shirt, the shirt felt happy and felt like it was born for him.

Subesh went to the interview. He groomed well and spoke confidently. His communication was very clear, and the interviewers were impressed with him. He passed his interview and was selected.

His interview result was half-decided yesterday when he selected the white shirt. It was the white shirt's victory. When you have a successful person and a positive attitude, you will definitely win.

The Joining day , Subesh Wore the White shirt. Whenever Subesh wears the shirt, it feels very happy. Every day it expects that Subesh will come and choose it. If he does, it feels that was its day. On the other side, this shirt became his favorite shirt. He always wears this shirt for his important occasions.

The white shirt feels proud and tells its fellow shirts in the cupboard that it is the king of that cupboard because Subesh always takes more care of this shirt. Even though he wears some different shirts, he always gives a look into this shirt. That look made the white shirt proud.

There was an untold bonding happened between Subesh ad the white shirt. Once his cousin asked this white shirt for an interview, Subesh refused to give this shirt as he feel this is a lucky one for him.

Subesh's daily routine went well. Six months gone, Subesh removed two shirts from his cupboard, one blue and the other red, as they got faded. The white shirt became more bright because of its happiness. That day was White Shirt's day. Subesh took the shirt and wore it. He went to his boss home. His boss returned from China and called for a get together in his home.

White Tea:

Subesh's boss offered to drink a White Tea. White tea is a rarest variety of tea available in china. Different types of tea (white, yellow, green, oolong, dark, black) come from the same two main tea plant varieties but are processed differently to achieve different levels of oxidation. Black tea is the most oxidized, while white tea is the least. Even though it is named as white tea , it looks brown.

Subesh tasted the tea and he liked it very much. His boss understood this and offered him 2 half-kilogram packets of tea. The boss needs more understanding of his team despite how strong he is. If he has a good understanding of his team members, he never fails despite how weak he is. Because a team always wins. Subesh boss was perfectly doing this.

Subesh felt very happy and collected the white tea. As his boss gifted this, he felt more proud and happy with that tea.

The Next page of beautiful emotions was opened-Possesiveness. The white shirt noticed this and started fighting with the white tea. The white shirt started to show its seniority. The White Tea started defending as it is latest and precious to subesh.

Subesh drank white tea daily. He wears a white shirt on occasions only.

The tea started teasing the shirt. It told the shirt, "See, Subesh likes me more than you. That's why he is drinking me daily."

The white shirt was senior and could not control its ego. Immediately, it replied to the tea to shut its mouth, "I know he is drinking you daily. After some days, he will consume you fully and there will be no opposition after that, and I was waiting for that day."

After these words ,the tea realized that ending and it was true. It did not have any words to reply. So, it accepted its defeat and kept calm. The shirt's ego got satisfied by the tea's defeat. After that, the tea did not utter a word against the shirt.

The tea and shirt started counting the days. The tea was unable to enjoy its happiness. It was feeling bad to tease the shirt on that day because of that, it realized its end. If we came to know our end date, we cannot enjoy the remaining days. Each and every second will become hell. The same happened to the tea.

The Judgement Day:

And that final day came. The white shirt was enjoying the mourning day. Subesh was preparing for an important meeting. He wore the white shirt and asked his mom for tea. The last cup of tea was prepared. It was the last day for the tea. The white shirt is about to give re-entry in its permanent zone, and the tea is about to leave.

The tea does not want to leave Subesh, but no options, it has to leave, and the shirt has to take its place.

The tea was hot, and the vapors were coming out of the tea. These vapors are the finest form of the tea's tears. The vapors were touching the shirt, and the shirt ignored them. What a cruelty!

Subesh was drinking the tea sip by sip. The white shirt was looking at the tea and started laughing. The tea was almost at its end. The tea is decided and accepted its end.

But it does not want to leave the space to the shirt. Before the final sip, the tea spilled on the shirt. The white shirt became **The White Tea shirt.**

The Judgement:

After the spill of tea, the shirt became useless as it held the stain of tea. Unnecessary ego and unwanted clashes spoil everything.

The tea did not live properly in its lifetime, and the shirt enjoyed that. When the day started for the shirt, it was unable to live now. Karma revolves everywhere. When both were in good shape, they fought each other and did not realize the value of themselves. Now, both are together and become useless for anybody. What an irony!

Subesh tried to clear the stain on the shirt, but the tea shade refused to go.

Finally, Subesh threw the shirt away. His mom took it and used it to clean light dust. Once the dust collected together in the shirt, she started using it to clean kitchen stains. Stains started sticking to the shirt. She used it to mop the floor. After some days of use, the white, shirt, tea, and everything were gone, and it became a torn, stained cloth.

On the final day, it was thrown away from the home. The same with our life, how pure we are, it doesn't matter. Once the stain of ego comes, it cannot go and collects other stains also, and finally, life becomes useless.

After the ending of the white, tea and shirt, they realized the truth together and started speaking to each other.

The tea told the shirt, "Sorry, I should not have spilled on you. I have entirely spoiled everything."

The shirt replied to the tea, "I should have given way to you. I should not have been the barrier for you. I spoiled your lifetime. That's where everything started. At least if possible, Fogive me. I am sorry."

The White Tea shirt:

It was a winter day. The torn cloth lay on the street. A dog came near the cloth and grabbed it in its mouth. The shirt and tea inside the cloth smiled together and accepted their final journey. The dog ran down the street with the cloth in its mouth. While the dog ran, both of them were remembering the beautiful days with Subesh. Before the memories ended, the dog dropped the cloth near a very poor man who lived in the temporary sheds of the street.

What happened was this: The poor man had nobody and lived on the streets with his dog. He was shivering in the cold. The dog realized that his owner was shivering and started finding a solution. It smelled the torn cloth on the street, and the rest of the things happened.

The poor man saw the cloth with gratitude and thanked his dog by gently touching its head. He covered himself with the stained cloth and felt a relaxation from the cold.

Now, there is No ego - No quarrel - No white - No tea - No shirt, and No cold.

The shared love between the dog and the old man remains still alive.

"To love without condition, to talk without intention, to give without reason, to care without expectation, that is the spirit of true love"

II

GOOD FOOD

Bombay:

That was a beautiful rainy day in Mumbai.

Sivanesh landed at Mumbai Airport. He was traveling from Chennai to Mumbai for official work. After a usual delay of two hours, the flight landed at Mumbai Airport.

Sivanesh was feeling hungry due to the delay in the flight. He ordered a burger at the airport outlet. He loves burgers very much. Whenever he takes a bite of a burger, he loves the feel of crispiness in the patty, crunchiness in the lettuce and onion, softness in the bun, and smoothness in the mayonnaise and sauce. Particularly, he doesn't like cheese. He prefers burgers without cheese. He chews all these items and eats with a feeling that can be seen on his face.

After a quick bite of the burger, he booked a taxi to Andheri, where his company's head office is located. He reached Andheri in 20 minutes due to light traffic. It was a one-day plan for him. He started the work for which he had come. He met Pradmesh, who is in charge of his work. As he arrived late at the office, he skipped lunch and continued with his work. Pradmesh also understood the situation and cooperated with Sivanesh. Around three o'clock, they finished their work.

Hungry:

After finishing the work, both of them felt hungry. The brain is a big illusionist. It always keeps the things in front of your mind that you like and are interested in doing, and it hides the rest. In the same way, it hid their hunger and kept them busy until the work was finished. Once the work was completed, the hunger feeling came in FIFO (First In First Out) mode.

Pradmesh took Sivanesh to the nearest cafeteria. As it was post-noon, meals were not available. Both of them decided to have a quick bite.

"Shivji, what would you like to have?" Pradmesh asked Sivanesh.

"Can we get a burger here?" Sivanesh replied.

"Why not, ji? Mumbai has all the things you want," Pradmesh replied with a laughter tone.

"Then I will have a burger," Sivanesh finalized his order.

Pradmesh went to the shopkeeper and started talking in Marathi.

"Kākā, ēkaz bargar āṇi ēkaz vaḍā pāva. Vaḍā pāva āhēs nā?" ("Uncle, one burger and one vada pav. You have vada pav, right?") He asked for a burger and one vada pav to the shopkeeper.

The shopkeeper replied, "Tū, asa kasa sāṅgitalansa? Hī mumba'āhē, vaḍāpāvaśivāya jagaṇāra kasē?"

"How did you say that? This is Mumbai, without vada pav, how will we live?" The shopkeeper replied.
Mumbai may live without air and water, but not without vada pav.

After placing the order, Pradmesh came to Sivanesh. Sivanesh was busy on his mobile phone. He noticed Pradmesh. He said to the other person on the phone, "Sir, Pradmesh is also with me. I will put the phone on speaker, we will finish the issue over the call." He kept the phone on the table.

Pradmesh shook his head and accepted. Both started speaking to the person on the phone. The conversation started.

BG & VP:-

After five minutes, two plates were served on the table.

One with a burger (BG) and the other one with a vada pav (VP).

BG and VP looked like a big brother and a small brother.

VP started speaking to BG, "Hey bro, how are you?"

The big giant BG heard the voice and started searching here and there and found this little giant near him.

"You little champ, why are you calling me bro? You may be a look-alike of me, but I cannot be your brother," BG shouted.

"Bro, I am not a look-alike. I am an invention and I have an inventor. I was born because of a shortage. Don't call me look-alike fatty," VP replied in Mumbai style.

"Hey, mind your words and don't blabber," BG defended.

"I'm not blabbering. Do you know your place of birth?" VP questioned BG.

BG thought for a second and told, "Yeah, I was born in this cafe."

VP teased BG, "Oh, pity pretty baby, I am also born in this cafe. I am not asking this, where is your origin?"

BG started thinking again. "My origin? Maybe in the USA or Germany?"

"USA or Germany?" VP hooked BG.

"Maybe Germany," BG replied with a doubt.

"See, you are saying maybe, so you do not know the exact origin. I was born in Mumbai, earlier Bombay," VP proudly replied.

"OK," BG replied in a soft manner.

"Do you know who invented you?" Again VP asked.

"Seriously, I don't know," BG replied in a tone that it did not want a battle.

"I was invented by Ashok Vaidya in 1966," again VP replied proudly.

"What? It means you have a story for that?" BG asked surprisingly.

"Yes. It is not my story. It is his story," with Mumbai style.

"What?" BG didn't understand.

"History," VP replied with a high-pitched tone.

"We both do not have time. They are going to eat us in a few minutes," BG tried to stop VP.

"They will not come for the next ten minutes. You didn't listen to their conversation. It will take at least ten minutes to convince their client," VP was very confident.

BG agreed to hear the history. "OK, go ahead."

HISTORY:

VP began, "Imagine, in the 1960s, a person named Ashok Vaidya, inspired by Shri Balasaheb Thackeray's call for Maharashtrians to become entrepreneurs, opened a small shop outside Dadar railway station. He sold Poha and Batata Wada.

Poha is an Indian breakfast made with flattened rice, onions, spices, herbs, lemon juice, and peanuts.

Batata Wada is a fried snack of batter-coated potato fritter dumplings mixed with chopped green chili, garlic, mustard seeds, and spices (also known as Bonda in South India).

Near him, a fellow colleague was selling Omlete Pav, a bun stuffed with an egg omelet.

On August 23, 1966, at the omelet pav shop, the eggs ran out, and the seller, with customers waiting, didn't know what to do. He sought help from Vaidya.

At Vaidya's shop, the Poha had finished, but he had Vadas.

An idea struck Vaidya. He stuffed the Vada inside the Pav and sold it to the customers. His intention wasn't to sell but to satisfy the customer's hunger. The combination of the soft Pav and the crunchy, spicy Vada was a hit. Customers asked for more.

The true success of good and tasty food is when someone asks for 'One More.'

That's where my journey began. From the next day, instead of Batata Wada, he started selling Vada Pav, and it became a success. Many people started Vada Pav shops in Mumbai.

I am an affordable Food that is easily accessible to a common man.

I became one of the best-selling items in Mumbai and Maharashtra. Today, you can find Me everywhere, from street vendors to sophisticated food malls.

See I am holding a place near to you" VP Finished.

BG got stunned by hearing his story (History) " Hats off to you buddy, I do not know you have a such history, I need to search for mine"

"Obviously you too may have a history... It's time for our duty , lets ready to die Come" VP Noticed that they had finished the call.

Sivnesh was about to take the burger. But he noticed this little giant and asked Pradmesh "Is it a mini burger?"

Pradmesh smiled and said "No, No , It is not mini burger, it Vada Pav "

Sivnesh asked with a doubtfully " What is Vada Pa?"

"I can say , it is called as Bombay Burger" Pradmesh replied.

A Curiosity came to shivnesh mind and asked " If you don't mine can i try this?"

"Yeah sure " Pradmesh offered the Vada pav to sivnesh

Sivnesh took a bite of the Vada Pav, which was filled with Batata Vada, garlic chutney, fried corn flakes, small pieces of onion, and fried chili. The soft Pav, spicy garlic chutney, corn flakes, and the divine taste of Vada and chili created magic on his tongue. The enjoyment of the taste was evident on his face. He finished the entire Vada Pav.

BG watched Sivnesh's reaction and thought, 'I wish I could have been born as VP.'

After finishing the Vada Pav, Sivnesh asked Pradmesh, "Can I get one more, please?"

* * *

Vada Pav is an affordable snack that is easily accessible to a common man. Today, more than 1.67 million Vada Pavs are sold in a day in Mumbai. It's a market worth approximately 1000 crores in Mumbai and 2000 crores in India. August 23 is celebrated as 'Vada Pav Day.'

Beyond the business, the idea that came to solve the hunger of a common man truly deserves a royal salute.

I dedicate this story to Shri Ashok Vaidya, who invented this wheel, and to the trillions of Vada Pavs that have satisfied and satisfying the hunger of common people in this country.

At the end of this story, As a dedication I am renaming the title to

"THE BOMBAY BURGER"

"A recipe has no soul. You, as the cook, must bring soul to the recipe."

III
THIRD DIMENSION

There will be always two dimensions in a debate.
First dimension: People who are trying to oppose the content.
Second dimension: People who are supporting the content.
There is a third dimension and I am going to tell you that.

First Dimension:

A 32-inch television mounted in the top corner of a small restaurant in New Delhi is displaying news channels with its high-decibel sound. A news reader is delivering her full sound to inform the public of the latest news.

"Air horns are banned in the city as noise pollution is increasing inside the city. Soon, it will be implemented in other parts of the nation as well."

Noise - What is meant by noise? Anything with more decibels is noise. The sound of an engine in a car, trains, and trucks. Disturbing sounds from horns in the streets. Morning wake-up alarms. Emergency alarms from a hooter, vibration of a motor. Human voices in the market.

All these sounds are called noise.

I am one of these things that generates noise.

I was manufactured in Tamil Nadu and am now in transit to Gujarat. People are trying to put a ban on me because I am creating noise. There are two dimensions to thia story. First dimension: People are trying to put a ban on me. Second dimension: There are people who are involved in my manufacturing process, and their livelihoods depend on me. There is a third dimension and I am going to tell you that.

Still thinking, who am I?

I am giving you a clue. I creates Sound...

Still thinking?

I Creates light also...

Still thinking...

No worries, Let me give a self introduction...

Second Dimension

I am a 1000-wala garland cracker, which explodes itself and expresses the celebration of others. I die in a small explosion, but my death ignites a lot of smiles. Come, let me give you a detailed introduction about myself.

Myself - I am not the complete 1000-wala. I am one among the thousand crackers tied up together to form a garland of electrical crackers. I am the 3-inch version of the garland cracker variants.

I was manufactured by the hands of people in Sivakasi, a district full of cottage industries in South Tamil Nadu. For a one-day Diwali celebration in India, this district manufactures crackers throughout the year. There are no formal or heavy machineries for manufacturing us.

Papers are processed at some locations. Aluminum, potassium, and sulfur are processed at different locations and converted into powders. Small cardboard tubes are manufactured at some locations, and threads are manufactured at different locations.

At some houses, the powders are mixed and filled inside the cardboard tubes. It is covered with paper, and gunpowder threads are inserted into the filled tube. The outer layer of the tube is pasted with red paper. Then it becomes a single firecracker, and that is me. This house will make thousands of single firecrackers in a day.

Everything will be transported to another house. There, they knot the crackers together and form a garland. This will be packed into a single pack.

Before lightening the celebration in one's hand, this one single cracker lightens the needs and livelihoods of more than 10 houses and 100 hands.

Third Dimension:

I have crossed 4 states and reached here after a week-long journey in this truck. It is for a marriage celebration. A lot of fireworks are ordered, and there are multiple numbers of skyliner crackers ordered, which fly from the earth and burst in the sky. The garland I am residing in is the one and only unique piece they have bought. Rest all are skyline crackers.

I don't know why they have brought us here. Is it a mistake or a wrong delivery? I don't know.

We are in the godown for a day. The next day—no, no, no, it is night. All the skyline fireworks are taken.

They have started firing one by one. I have heard the sounds of the crackers that died in the air, and humans are celebrating our death.

How cruel they are. The sounds of the crackers are really painful to me, more than that, the sounds of humans who clapped and whistled while the crackers were burned. I am getting angry at this. What to do? Some humans manufactured us for their livelihood, and some humans are killing us for their celebration.

The next day, one guy came and took us. We are on his shoulders and traveling from the godown to somewhere. He was walking away from the godown and reached the garden of that big bungalow. He took us towards the gate and dropped us on the ground. There was a big, costly seven-seater SUV standing near us.

One guy came and shouted to the one who dropped us, "Don't put the cracker near the car. It is a costly gift for the marriage. Don't spoil it. Keep it away from this and light the car when the bride and groom are starting the car."

The poor guy took and kept us in a distance and waited for the arrival of the bride and groom. Now I have understood we are here to celebrate the arrival of the costly car. We are worthless in front of this now. As per humans' point of view, value will change as per the thing in front of themselves.

My ego got hurt. I don't want to die for this kind of happiness.

I have made a decision now, and I am not going to burst in this celebration. I don't care about the 999 tied along with me, but I don't want to die.

The bride and groom came. The garland was lit with a fired matchstick. The matchstick was thrown away after lighting the thread, it died. But it got its next birth (the Punar Janma) in the thread and started spreading to the crackers. Crackers are not able to withstand this Punar Janma. Each and everyone started bursting continuously. Much and much noise. I escaped from this group burst, but I was thrown away in the heat burst of nearby crackers. I have started flying in the air due to the pressure and somewhere I have fallen down. I am unable to see anything.

Full of smoke, and I think I am fainting now and I have fainted completely.

Punar Janma (Re-Birth):

I can see now. I am on the roadside platform. All my colleagues are dead. Crackers have become paper now. All are awaiting the cleaning team. I was looking around. Most of them are dead and became pieces of paper. Some of them are semi-busted and they are also dead. I am the only survivor in this clash.

A small girl was sitting on the roadside, searching something between these papers. She took the half-burned crackers and collected them in her small plastic bag. She was not like the humans who were yesterday. She wore a dusty cloth with dark-toned skin. People who were walking on the road were keeping a distance while crossing her path. She found me and took me in her hands. She found that I am alive.

She threw a smile. What a smile it is! A smile with 200% happiness. Her face was very beautiful in that smile. Yesterday, the claps and whistles for the 300-foot flying skyline crackers failed in front of her smile for a single 3-inch cracker. It lit an infinite illumination on her face. I am happy now and the reason is her happiness. The real happiness always spread from one place to other.

She took me to her home and started her celebrating process. She took all the metal powders in the half-burned crackers. A teaspoon of powder was collected. She formed a thin line using the powders and kept me at the end of the line. My thread was touching the line.

I have understood. My death process had started. What a way of celebrating with a semi busted crackers. I am happy to die for her smile and her happiness. I felt that a like music in between this noise.

She lit the starting point of the line with a matchstick. I got enlightened. The fire started in the powder line and spreading forward and I was waiting for my turn and i was continuously watching the happiness on her face. The fire line is on its way towards me. I am in firing mode now. Come and catch me Let me die for a cause.

Suddenly, she came fast and moved me away from the line. The fire got completed at the end of line and It did not touch me. She took me and started running. I got confused. She went to her mom and said some thing and put me in her Mom's Hand and ran away to play on the street side.

What she told was "Maa, I will crack this for Diwali, till then save this for me."

Hey Kiddo, I am a single drop out piece from the garland, I can produce a small level of light and noise, but it is going to create an unlimited happiness on your face, At that time I may not be alive to see that.

Still I am waiting for that day.

"Be happy with the little what you have. There are people with nothing and still smiling with what they have."

""

""

IV
SUBSTITUTE

The Story:

Kapilesh a 48-year-old chemical engineer who works in a factory in Hyderabad. He was planning to write a book about the learnings in his life. He started his career as a 10th-grade-passed helper in that chemical company's lab 30 years ago. He learned about chemicals by helping his seniors and studied part-time for a diploma. He was promoted to lab assistant from helper. Later, he did B.Sc. Chemistry and was promoted to chemical engineer in the same company. He completed 30 years in that company. He thought of writing his experiences into a book and started doing so.

Actually, this book-writing idea was given by his son, Ganesh. Ganesh is studying engineering in telecommunications. He suggested his dad write a book about his experiences. Kapilesh agreed and started working on it.

Kapilesh bought a new laptop for his writing. Until then, he did not have any computer at home. He always used his office computer for all internet-related activities. Now he used his smartphone. For writing, he had considered buying a desktop computer, but Ganesh suggested buying a laptop as it would be helpful for portability. Along with a laptop, he also bought a wireless mouse as he was not familiar with using the laptop's trackpad.

The Failure:

One fine day, he started writing. Actually, he started typing. He used the mouse for cursor positioning and started typing his story on the laptop. As he was new to writing, the Backspace button was the most typed button on his keyboard. In most writing tasks, the space bar is usually the most hit key compared to others. However, in his case, it was entirely opposite. He mostly pressed Backspace as he was not satisfied with what he was writing.

With increasing complexity, he completed three chapters with a page count of 45, containing 8,000 words, 7,999 spaces, and an unknown number of backspace hits. In cricket, more hits increase the run rate. In writing, more hits can decrease the keyboard's lifespan. Yes, his keyboard's backspace did not work properly. Unfortunately, this keyboard layout does not have two backspace keys, but it has two Ctrl, two Shift, and two Alt keys.

Keyboards simplify life. We need control to do anything in life, we need to shift if we are not doing something correctly, and Either a plan or a thing we always need an alternate to do something unstoppable. Ctrl , Shift and Alternate are the things we need in our life and the keyboard has two of all. There is no more space for backspace.

Kapilesh asked Ganesh, "Gane, the backspace isn't working on my keyboard. Can you please check it?"

"Two minutes nana , I will check it " He asked a maggi permission and kapilesh granted.

After twice the noodle cooking time, Ganesh came to check the keyboard. He pressed the backspace key, but it didn't work. He blew air around the backspace key and pressed it again, but it still didn't work. He removed the keycap, cleaned the key with a brush, and pressed it, but it still didn't work. Ganesh tried all these methods, but nothing worked. The failed key had won the battle. Ganesh accepted his defeat.

"Dad, I think we need to take this to a service center. Should I book a complaint and get it fixed tomorrow?" Ganesh asked his dad.

Kapilesh said, "Okay, I'll come with you to the service center tomorrow."

The next day, both reached the service center on Gachibowli Road. They explained the problem to the service center technician. He noted the serial number and checked the warranty date. Since it was under warranty, he agreed to examine the fault. After examination, he said, "Sir, the key is damaged. Keyboard problems generally aren't covered under warranty. So if you need it fixed, you'll have to replace the keyboard at your own cost."

Kapilesh understood the situation immediately and didn't argue with the technician. He politely asked, "What will be the cost of a replacement keyboard?"

"It will be 5,500 rupees, sir," the technician replied.

"Okay, please proceed with the keyboard replacement," Kapilesh confirmed and made an advance payment. The technician told them to wait for a few minutes in the reception while he replaced the keyboard.

Both sat on the sofa in the reception. After watching all this, Ganesh politely asked his dad, "Dad, why did you agree to the replacement? If we had argued with them for some more time, they might have given us a free replacement."

Kapilesh smiled and said, "See, this was my fault. I pressed that key many times, sometimes hard, out of frustration, which damaged the key. If we know the root cause of the problem, we should accept it and move on. Only then can we rise in life."

Ganesh's curiosity wasn't satisfied. He asked his dad, "Okay, Dad, now you found the root cause. However, due to writing, some keys might fail in the future as well. So will you keep changing the keyboard every time for 5,500 rupees?"

Kapilesh smiled again and said, "No. This is my first laptop, so I don't want any failures in it. I'm not going to use the keyboard."

Ganesh was curious. "Not going to use the keyboard? Then how will you write your story? Are you going to hire someone?"

Kapilesh smiled again and replied, "No. The solution is simple. I'll order a Bluetooth keyboard that I can connect to the laptop, just like I'm using a wireless mouse. Even if it fails, I can replace it again."

Ganesh understood and said, "You're a genius, Dad."

Kapilesh replied, "No, I'm a chemical engineer."

While sitting in the reception, Kapilesh searched for a keyboard on an e-commerce site and found a low-cost one with same-day delivery. He ordered it immediately.

Forty-five minutes later, the service technician gave the laptop back with the new keyboard. Kapilesh tested all the keys and found them to be working. They collected the laptop and returned home.

The KB:

That evening, the parcel arrived. Kapilesh opened it and found the low-cost keyboard with a battery. He inserted the battery, the keyboard powered on, and he connected it to the laptop. The keyboard was ready to use.

The keyboard powered on and started looking around. It found its neighbor, Mr. Mouse, who was dancing here and there.

The keyboard asked the mouse, "Hey Mousy, how are you? I'm KB."

Mousy looked at it and said, "KB? I think you're a keyboard."

"Yes, I am. Keyboard is my full form, and KB is my short form."

Mousy laughed and said, "Don't shorten your name. Keep your name a little longer because your life is going to be short." Mousy frightened the KB.

"What are you saying?"

Mousy explained the entire story to KB, and finally, KB understood that it was a substitute for the laptop keyboard's death game.

The Substitute:

The mission started for both KB and Kapilesh.

Day by day, the book started growing. KB had reached a point where the story had 3 chapters with 8,000 words. Now, the story had grown to 15 chapters with 35,000 words.

KB thought that Kapilesh was going to kill it for sure. But Kapilesh was as polite as always. He handled the keyboard gently, pressing the keys carefully. The keys made no sound, he handled it so softly.

Kapilesh learned one thing from his life: "Make mistakes, but never repeat them." He didn't have the habit of repeating mistakes. So, he took care of KB. Daily, he brushed the dust inside the keys. He covered the keyboard with a cloth after work was completed. He monitored the battery power and replaced it properly.

Not only because of the early failure, Kapilesh also became emotionally bonded with KB as it was helping him create a written form for his lifetime learnings. In other words, he was capturing his life moments through KB.

On the other side, KB read whatever Kapilesh wrote. KB became more curious to understand the daily story he wrote. By listening to Kapilesh's life story, a tree of respect for Kapilesh grew in KB's heart.

More than Kapilesh, KB was more eager to complete this book.

The flow for the book came perfectly. After typing for 7 months, Kapilesh was 99% completed with the book. He has decided to complete the last page tomorrow.

In the meantime, KB was discussing with Mousy.

"Mousy, I'm happy that Kapilesh is finishing his book."

"Why are you so happy, KB? It's his book he's completing. Why are you getting so excited about it?"

"It's his book, but I'm happy that I was a part of this good job."

"So what? You're not going to get credit for this. Luckily, none of your parts failed. Otherwise, you would have been fired immediately."

"Don't be so negative, Mousy. Even if I had failed today, I would have been happy because I died for completing this story. There is a purpose for my living."

KB had absorbed all the positivity from Kapilesh's fingers. He spoke like Kapilesh.

Mousy was not ready to accept this situation and said, "However, don't forget you're a cheap substitute keyboard from an e-commerce website."

KB ignored the negativity from Mousy. Drops of negativity melted in the sunshine of positivity.

The Final Words

Kapilesh started writing the final page. There was only one line to complete. The K and E keys on the KB got stuck. No output came.

Kapilesh started typing K and E, but it didn't work. KB tried to deliver the output, but it didn't come.

Kapilesh pressed again, but it didn't work. Mousy's words came true. KB was about to fail. But KB didn't want its master to fail. It collected all its power and put it into the K and E keys. It was praying that Kapilesh should type the key again.

God listened to KB's prayer. Kapilesh pressed the key, and the output came. Kapilesh finished his final line.

But something came to Kapilesh's mind, and he started typing the next line. KB was shocked. It didn't have further power to save itself. What to do? It wanted Kapilesh to win.

Again, it collected all its power and prepared for the next line. It didn't have further strength to hold on. If Kapilesh typed again, KB would die for sure because it had exhausted its entire life during this period. Still, it wanted its master to win and stood ready for the last line.

Kapilesh entered the keys one by one. All of KB's power went into those words, and at the end of the full stop, KB ended its life at the end of line.

The Real KB:

KB ended its life for Kapilesh's book. You do your good job, and the results will reap automatically.

Kapilesh named his book "The Kapil's Book," shortened to "The KB."

"The KB" was released in the market and did well. It became one of the bestsellers in the market.

Years passed. After 25 years, "The KB" broke all market records. The great author Kapilesh passed away.

To pay tribute to Kapilesh, his belongings were kept in a museum. People came to see those things. In that list, the most visited item was the KB, the keyboard used to type the book "The KB." It was kept there because the last line of the book was,

"I really thank this keyboard that helped me type this book. I hadn't decided on the title for the book so far. Now, in this last line, I am giving the title of the book. To show my gratitude to 'The Kapil's Book' and the keyboard that helped me type this book, this book will be called 'The KB.' "

"Always perform your duty effieciently an without attachement to the results, becuase by doing the work without attachement one reaches The Supreme" - *Bagavath Gita*

V

SHARP LOVE

The Knife Story

I was born in Burma in 1975. I am a handcrafted piece, made with Chromium vanadium alloy 6000 Series Steel and a Burman Teak wood handle.

I am 2 inches wide and 1 foot long, including the 4-inch handle.

I am designed for cutting Vegetable - Sorry A small correction I am used for cutting vegetables.

I was owned by Maruthesh, a renowned Chettinad chef in the mid-south east districts of Tamil Nadu. His father bought me in Burma while working there and gifted me to Maruthesh.

He loved and respected me greatly. He would touch me and perform a Namaskar before starting work. He always performed a puja before work, and I deserved a place in it.

When Maruthesh began cooking for a function, people in and around the area could easily identify his presence by the aroma of the food being prepared. People also eagerly watched his beautiful and stylish way of cutting vegetables.

When he took me in his hand, we both became enthusiastic. I always produced a rhythm when cutting vegetables. When slicing a thick piece, I created a "Sssshk" sound, and when slicing a thin piece, I created a "tuk" sound. The rhythm of "ssshks" and "tuks" determined the size of the slice.

For large potato fries, I would make 5 "ssshks" - 4 horizontal and 1 vertical. For breakfast sambar potatoes, I would make 8 "ssshks" and 10 "tuks" - 8 vertical and 10 horizontal.

ssshk ssshk ssshk ssshk ssshk ssshk ssshk sshhk tuk tuk tuk tuk tuk tuk tuk tuk tuk

In just a few seconds, a large 2-inch potato could be transformed into 160 pieces.

He was a fast and furious version of vegetable cutting.

The decibel of my sound indicated my sharpness to my master. If my rhythm was not perfect, he would sharpen me. However, this didn't happen often.

After all the work was done, he would keep me in a wooden box made with Burman Teak wood.

"Precious things deserve precious places."

The Love Story

I am not alone. I have a pair. The wooden box was designed for two knives. I am one half, and she is my better half. If I am the king, she is the queen. She is a little smaller than me but sharper in performance. My master uses her only for puja-related tasks.

She is used to cut flower garlands, threads, fruits, sandalwood, vibhuti, and kumkum packets for pujas. These are all very small tasks compared to her sharpness. She often complains to me about this.

"I don't know why our master uses me only for very small tasks. Look at my sharpness. My performance is not utilized properly," she complains to him in a sad tone.

"Don't worry about that. You are used for puja-related tasks, which are precious. He dedicates you to these tasks. He never uses me for puja work, so you are very precious to him," he calms her with a polite voice.

"That's not my problem. My concern is that we are unable to work together," she worries again.

Love always wants the pair together becuase it was made for eachother.

After hearing this, he creacked a joke "Wait! I will imagine How can he cut vegetables with two knives in hand? who will hold the the potatoe now?"

"Oh, is that a joke? I'll laugh tomorrow. Please remind me," she teases him.

"Okay, I'll remind you," he replies.

She continues, "Do you know, I love the way you pierce vegetables. I am mesmerized by the rhythmic sound. I would like to be close or near you in the rhythm." She was pouring out her love for him.

When we start loving someone, we begin to notice their every movement and love to relive those moments. Similarly, she registered every nanosecond of the Vegetable piercing in her mind.

He quietly listens to her conversation and replies, "Do you think I don't miss you? Everyone's path is destined for a certain job. I am happy here. We are made for each other, and this wooden box is proof."

"Yes, I know. Let us enjoy the moment we have"

"Now you are my girl."

Yes, they were made for each other, and the wooden box was their home and Marudesh was the God for them.

The Sharp Story:

It was an auspicious day. Marudesh was cooking for a family function in a marriage hall. He performed the puja and kept the small knife in the wooden box.

He lit the camphor and fired the wooden stove. He began cutting the white pumpkin for the sambar. Taking the knife, he punctured the top of the pumpkin and inserted the knife about six inches deep. With a push, the knife quickly sliced the pumpkin in half. He rotated the pumpkin 90 degrees and repeated the process on the other side. The pumpkin was divided into two pieces in less than a minute.

She watched the knife's journey through the pumpkin. She loved the clean cuts and the tiny sparks that flew during the cutting. Marudesh was a master at handling vegetables gently. If they had lives, they would not feel the pain of being cut.

Although he handled vegetables with care, he was not as skilled at dealing with people. He was a master chef but not a people person. On that day, he was shouting at one of his assistants for not doing a job properly.

They argued back and forth. At the height of the argument, the assistant used a vulgar word against Marudesh. Already at his Peak anger, Marudesh was triggered by the insult.

He immediately threw the knife at the assistant. Fortunately, the knife missed its target and fell to the ground, In another words he saved his master.

Enraged by the knife-throwing incident, the assistant ran towards Marudesh, jumped on him, and slapped him. Marudesh lifted the assistant and threw him to the ground. The assistant landed on his back. Marudesh turned the assistant over and sat on him. He grabbed the other knife from the wooden box. He raised the knife over his shoulder, pointed it at the assistant's chest, and prepared to strike.

She had always wanted to cut a vegetable; now, she was about to kill a human being.Her pair watched the scene from a distance, unable to understand what was happening.

She was moving towards the ground, and the assistant was near to kill. She was rarely used ad she was shining brightly. Its reflection caught Marudesh's eye, and he realized that he was about to kill someone.

He got his consiouness banck and immediately dropped the knife.

The killing was stopped. As she fell to the ground, she breathed a sigh of relief.

But her relief was short-lived. She felt herself being lifted.

Yes The assistant had picked up the knife. Before she could react, he plunged the knife into Marudesh's neck, She Penrated the skin and cut his windpipe and blood vessels. The assistant released the knife, and Marudesh fell to the ground with the knife still embedded in his neck.

Sharp Love:

After a few minutes, he died. The guy got arrested by the police. On the one side she holds the blood of his master and the other side she holds the finger print of his enemy. She baecame the murder weapon. Police took the knife and kept it in the Jail's treasury. The wooden box and the other knife were taken by the incharge of the Marriage Hall and Knife is cutting the fruits, Threads, Flower garlands And other puja items. He was continuing her work with his Sharp loving memory. He still remembers the day of killing

When she pierced her master's neck, she was between the master and the enemy. She was between the master and the enemy in two situations.

The first time, she was in her master's hand, and the enemy was on the opposite side. No killing occurred.

The second time, she was in the enemy's hand, and the master was on the opposite side. She killed her own master.

We should not drop our good things. As long as we hold them in our hands, they protect us and prevent us from doing bad things. If we let go of them and allow them to fall into the wrong hands, they can turn harmful. They are good because they are in our hands.

Similarly, emotions are like that. If they are beautiful, they create a beautiful environment for ourselves and those around us. When Marudesh was in control of his emotions, he and she were happily together.

When Marudesh lost control of his emotions and turned bad, it led to terrible consequences. Marudesh died, and the man went to jail. What were the mistakes made by the beautiful pair of knives? They were separated. She is in the jail became rusty due to the feeling of separation. He became a truly inanimate object, unaware of what it was cutting daily. The beautiful love was alone and it has nobody to share.

Without the knowledge of all these things the wooden box become the stationary box to the kid of the Marriage Hall incharge who took the knife and Box. Instead of the knife it gave accomadation to pencil, pen and eraser. The box is daily going to school along with the kid.

I am happy that it at least had a chance to receive some education among these educated but uncontrolled emotional people.

"The cause of anger rarely hurts us as much as the consciousness of anger"

VI
EXPRESSION

She:

"I always felt that he and me were born for each other. I don't know our manufacturing dates, but we know for what purpose we were born. He always tells me that we were born to take people from one place to another. Without us, they can't travel. But our presence is very important in their lives. Our ancestors invented us in rocks. Later, we got our formation in woods and then in steel and now in rubber. Yes, we are the tires, the circumference of the wheels.

Myself and himself are the tires of scooters. We are in the store of this scooter company. I met him a day ago when I was being packed into a truck. He was placed near me, and I fell in love with him. Falling in love at first sight isn't just for humans; it's applicable for us as well. The moment I saw him, I started to feel the atoms of original latex inside me. His presence triggered the memories of when I was flowing through the rubber tree. Even after a lot of chemical processes, he made me feel the originality of mine. This might be our form of Dopamine, oxytocin, and serotonin rush in our system. Who knows?

He:

"Yes! She was telling the truth. The moment I entered the truck, I saw her and started feeling the white color in my skin instead of my processed black. The packaging guy was pushing me into the truck. I hit her and fell down. When I touched her, I started traveling back to my life in the rubber trees in Kerala. I heard a lot of love stories and witnessed a lot of love chemistry between people when I was in the form of a tree. Even during my cultivation, transportation, and in processing factories, I have witnessed a lot of human love stories.

For me, humans are the gods of love. When I see people who are in love, I can feel their love while they are handling me. In the rubber tree farm, during my extraction process, the guy who carries me in his hand and sees his lover girl, gives a smile and passes me in a second. That particular second he passes me her way; I felt some kind of softness in his hand. Love is the one and only compound that creates a chemical reaction in all of the particles in this earth. Similarly, I have witnessed a lot of love stories, and at the final moment, I have also faced the same."

Love:

"The truck started traveling from a south district to a north district of Tamil Nadu. It would take almost a day to reach the factory. Two of the tires were among the 500 tires in the truck. Don't know about the feeling of others, but these two shared their feelings in the truck and exchanged their hearts.

He started chatting with her, 'Hi, where are you going?'

'I am going to the USA, and you are going to the UAE,' she teased him. But she enjoyed it internally, at least he had initiated the conversation.

'Yes, it's a good joke,' he appreciated her.

'Will you not laugh if it's a bad one?' she made a counter-question.

'I will,' he replied smartly. This reply cracked a smile between these two, and a lovable conversation between both of them started from there.

The tires felt like rotating without the wheels. It took 15 hours to reach the two-wheeler manufacturing unit from the tire factory. They started speaking about their origin, locations they were born, the people who handled them, process methods, and everything they had crossed in their lives.

The chemical reaction that happened between each other consisted of a lot of new formulas that even scientists and engineers couldn't invent.

"Both of them understood each other and came into sync of minds.

She continued the conversation, "When will this truck reach the factory?'

He thought for a second and told, "It's a small truck, so it will be traveling a short distance, maybe a maximum of one day."

After hearing this, she became sad.

"We should have been born as bigger truck tires," she replied.

He got confused and asked, "I didn't understand."

"We both will be together as a pair of wheels. We were born as two-wheeler tires and we don't even have a chance to be together,"there was a pain in her words. She continued,"At least they should have kept the factory a little longer. We may have spent time together."

He understood the situation and tried to explain to her, "We are born for servicing others. We don't have our own life, and you need to accept this irony."

He also understood that this would be over in a few hours and prepared his mind for that.

Separation:

The truck reached the factory, and the tires were ready to unload. She was feeling sad. An operator loaded the tires one by one and kept them in a hanging trolley.

The trolleys were moved inside the factory to assemble. All the tires were mounted on the wheel and fixed in a production line trolley. These tires were ready for the assembly sequence. If two stars were not shining in the sky, how would it look? Both of them were like that. Inside that machine of life, nobody cared about themselves or their bonding.

These kinds of components were moved into the factory to give birth to two-wheelers, which creates a new beginning. All the tires were excited for this new journey, but these two tires were feeling like they were traveling towards their end.

Both were entered into the production line. It was a moving line. A scooter assembled without wheels came in the conveyor belt. He was in front, and she was next to him. An operator took him for assembly on the scooter. Both were nervous at the end of the moment. He tried to look at her in the back and slipped from the operator's hand, falling to the ground. That operator didn't know what to do. He left the fallen tire and took the next one, which was herself. She was watching this and didn't understand what had happened in these few seconds. While the operator was fixing her on the wheel with pressure and starting to assemble as the front wheel of the scooter, unknowing all these things, she fainted.

Life:

A week later, a mechanic was spraying water on the scooter before its delivery. She came to consciousness. The scooter was delivered to a village. A farmer in the village received the scooter. He drove it through the Indian village roads, where the real battle for a two-wheeler begins. It traveled on many difficult roads in the villages.

She didn't feel anything. Her thoughts were completely focused on his memories. She didn't understand why he had fallen down. She didn't know where he was. She felt like she was living in an unknown universe.

She ran on the road for almost 5,000 kilometers, crossing many mud roads, stone paths, plains, and concrete roads. Nothing registered in her mind. All she could think about was him.

As she was the front tire, she didn't get any punctures because the man who drove the scooter always noticed thorns and stones on the road and turned the wheel accordingly. However, the rear tire got punctured frequently, and it happened again that day.

The tire mechanic found the rear tire unusable and removed it, replacing it with a new one. After removing the rear tire, he dropped it in front of the scooter.

She noticed this and was shocked because it was him. She saw his outline with more than ten puncture patches. He looked like a soldier with wounds, and indeed, he was.

Flash Back:

During the assembly of the wheel, he noticed that he was going to be assembled in the front wheel. If he was in the front wheel, obviously the next wheel would become the rear wheel, which was herself. He understood that if she became the rear wheel, she would be prone to get more punctures. He wanted her to live a long life, so he decided to slip off the operator's hand, so that in the production urgency, the operator would pick the next one and assemble it on the front wheel.

What he planned was executed. She became the front wheel, and he was picked next and assembled on the rear wheel. As she was in the front, she didn't know he was in the back.

As he had decided, he got all the punctures for her and sacrificed his life for love. It was an unexpressed love of him for her.

She understood all this and said in a painful voice, 'Until now, I was in pain that you were not with me. Henceforth, how should I live with guilt that you lost your life because of me? You must have told me this, at least I would be in a little satisfaction that you are behind me.'

He replied in a low-toned voice, "I thought at least you would live for a long time without pain. That's why I did this."

She heard him completely and replied, "I was ready to die with you in a few days instead of living a life without you."

Her last words stunned him, and he realized the mistake he had made. He had not expressed the love he had for her and that had hidden the reality in front of him.

The mechanic fixed the new wheel. The farmer started the scooter. The scooter was leaving with her in the front tire, and it was moving away from the sight of the removed tire, vanishing away like his unexpressed love for her.

" *Unexpressed Love is Never understood & Over Expressed love is never Valued* "

- Someone

ॐ

As an author I don't want to end the story like this. Let us explore the effect of the love expressed in the last moment

Re union:

The farmer took the scooter and drove for a day. As the rear tire was new and the front tire was old, he didn't have proper grip on the drive. It was also because of her. She knew where his partner was and she wanted to reach him. The only way was to get damaged. She didn't cooperate well, resulting in an uncomfortable drive for the farmer.

She hit a big, sharp stone and got a big puncture. The farmer took the scooter to the mechanic, who inspected it and told him that the size of the puncture was big and the tire would be unusable. The farmer agreed to change the tire.

He removed the front tire and changed it with a new one. He took the removed tire and threw it into the scrap yard.

She flew into the air, found him among the hundreds of scrapped tires, and fell on him. He realized that she was falling on him and was feeling very happy for her. These few months before, he had fallen on her in the truck and started a new love story. Now she had fallen on him, reinitiating the same story with the second chapter.

Chapter 2:

One day, a truck came. All the unused tires were collected in the truck. Similarly, it collected some more tires from other scrap yards.

The truck entered a Tire recycling factory, and they put all the tires in a big machine. That machine shredded the tires into small pieces, and the shredded pieces were processed for bitumen to lay the roads. Tires went inside the machine one by one. These two tires were bonded together;

they didn't want to separate from each other. They went inside the machine together.

Both of them were cut into pieces and mixed together. They got dissolved together and became one. It was processed into bitumen and laid on the road. They were reformed but were bonded together with love.

At first, they wanted to be together, because of their original forms, they didn't express thier love properly and created a chaos. Once they expressed and understood the love, they were ready to reform themselves for thier love. Finally They did for each other.

Even they are in different form and still they are together in love.

True love never fails. Even in a non-living thing, it lives forever.

"Where and how you live don't define your happiness. It's about who you're with?

Are you with your loved ones?

If So , are you expressing your love properly ?"

"The Principle is in Love, The detail is in how we express it "

&

VII

PEACE OF PIECE

In this Extra Large World, I am a Small piece, but I never find peace. When I was cotton, I was whipped by the air and heated by the sunlight. People invested money to cultivate me. They sold me for profit. There's nothing wrong with that. But I lost my freedom. Without a negative, a positive cannot exist. Atomic theory applies to everyone in the universe. So we must move on. I am in the same situation. My journey began here, and I am searching for peace.

There is hope that somewhere I will find peace and settle down.

The farmer sold me to a commission agent who collected cotton. Many cottons like me were born in our field and nearby fields, and we were gathered together in a warehouse. I was peacefully sleeping among the other cotton. The agent bought us from different farmers at different prices. He added and averaged the total price, added his margin, and sold us to a factory. My journey started again, I think peace to be found in the next stage.

They processed us together and turned us into pulp. Another relative joined our family: Mr. Linen. They mixed

20% of linen with us. Finally, we were converted into long, thin sheets. They named us paper, more specifically, 82 GSM paper. Technically, I weigh 82 grams per square meter with a thickness of 0.11 millimeters. I was carefully rolled into a cardboard tube and packed properly. I hoped I had found my place and would live peacefully.

I was loaded onto a truck. I thought my little time of peace was over. Again, they were going to do something to me. I was transported to a new location. They stored me in a temperature-controlled room with security cameras and double-level door protection. Not only that, there were armed guards for protection. Now I understood. This is called life: a safer and more secure place. Now my life was settled. Let me live peacefully.

After weeks of time, they started transporting us again. This time, it wasn't a solo journey. Within minutes, I had reached this place. I was in the form of a roll, and they mounted me on a cutting machine. This machine cut me into larger sheets. They applied some chemicals to me, then loaded me into a printing machine. It started printing on me on both sides multiple times. They then put me through a cutting machine again, which cut me into small pieces. I was searching for peace, but I had been turned into pieces. They collected my colleagues who had also been printed, bundled us together, and wrapped us and They named us 500 units value currency notes.

I understood now. My value had increased. Humans spend a maximum of a single-digit denomination upto 3 or 4 Units of money to manufacture me, but they valued me at 500 units, just because of the ink printed on me. I had simply masked my originality with ink, and my value had increased. Originality of Life is this!

Now humans would chase after me. Let us enjoy this peacefully.

We all moved to a box with the protection of two armed guards. We were moved to an ATM machine. My friends above me were collected and thrown out by the machine. I was waiting for my turn. It came. I was the only one who came out of the machine. A middle-aged man collected me from the machine and put me in his pocket. He was walking, and I was enjoying my first-time travel in a pocket. After a few seconds of walking, he took me out of his pocket and gave me to a Petrol Pump vendor, saying, "Next time, charge your card machine properly. I don't have time to go and collect money from the ATM every time. It doesn't mean that just because you have an ATM at your pump, you can tell us to collect money from the ATM for your mistake." After yelling at him, he started his car and drove away.

I was kept inside a cash bag. I could see many other currencies that looked like me. In fact, I was just like them.

I can smell the petrol around me. I don't like the irritating and slightly toxic smell. I was waiting to leave. That evening, the pump owner was giving weekly wages to the employee. I was one of the five currencies given to him. I was placed in his wallet. The wallet looked old but fresh. It seemed it wasn't used frequently or filled with guests like us frequently. He put the wallet in his back pocket. He took his bicycle and rode home. An employee of a petrol pump can't afford a petrol vehicle. After filling petrol for most vehicles in town, he drove a petrol-less vehicle. Another reality of life.

I felt uncomfortable traveling in the back seat. But I had to travel for at least 45 minutes. After reaching home, he took us from his wallet and placed us near the photo of God in his home. He worshiped me along with God. My value increased again. I was almost near to God now, just because of an ink. Paper doesn't have value, ink doesn't have value, but paper and ink together have value. It's the meaning of peace.

In a few minutes, a moneylender came to his home and asked for the interest on the money he had lent to them. Afraid of the lender, he gave three notes out of five to him, and I was one of them. We were loaded in his shirt pocket. Again, I was traveling in a shirt pocket. This time there was an upgrade. He wore a costly silk shirt. He reached his home and kept his shirt on the hanger. The petrol pump guy's home was a little hot, but this guy's home was fully air-conditioned. It seemed like a chilled day for me.

His son was asking money for video shoot. But he denies to give him and told you don't know the value of money. Now I understood the value of me.

The next day, There was an announcement happening in the TV that 500 units notes are Demonitised. It was a situation that non-accountable money are become use less. If they taken to bank they have to show accountablity for that. Money with the persons who deals un accountable activities are just become papers.After seeing that information the money lender realised that i will be no use for him.

He called his son,he took me out and gave it to him and told , "There is no value for this now, it is just piece of paper, do whatever you want." There would be no peace and I had to move on wherever these humans took me. I was traveling in all modes without a ticket reservation and was the only person humans didn't treat with untouchability. What to do? I became worse than a puppy dog that travels with its boss. A dog has its own boss, but I don't. After all these things I realized If I'm demonetized, I'm just a piece of paper "

The young boy folded me and put me inside his mobile cover. The most uncomfortable place for me, with more magnetic interference and a lot of heat dissipation. After a journey of two hours, he took me out, straightened me, held me in his hands in front of a mobile camera, and started speaking in front of the camera.

"Hi friends, do you know where we are and what we're going to do? In front of you, you can see a dead 500-unit currency note, and we're going to see the journey of the note. We're in the field of cotton where the currency was originally built."

Oh my God! I was searching for peace and finally came to the place where I originated. It means there is no peace, or am I missing something? I was looking into the fields carefully. The air was kissing the cotton buds, and the sun was clearing the wetness of the cotton buds. I didn't realize this before. I was traveling with the guy on his journey.

There was coolness in the process of creating the cotton pulp. I didn't realize this. There was an art of change that happened to us while they mixed with linen. I missed it.

There was rhythm when they rolled me in the cardboard tube. I missed it.

There were many villages and towns along the paths I crossed. I missed noticing them.

I didn't smell the aroma of the scented chemicals they added to me.

I didn't notice the face of the leader printed on me.

I didn't listen to the song played at the petrol pump.

In search of peace, I didn't realize anything and missed every small good thing in and around me, ending at the starting point without any value. Finally, I found that peace is inside me by enjoying the small moments and good things near me.

Don't search for peace. Realize it. It's inside you

""Peace Comes From Within ""

VIII
GAME

"Which one is the Most Watched Sport?"

If you asked this question in India, the answer would be Cricket.

Fifteen men inside the field: 11 from the playing team, 2 from the opposition, and 2 umpires for making decisions. 11 men from the playing team attempt to stop the opposing team from scoring runs.

Increasing numbers in the runs, falling of wickets, prediction of scores, run rate, half-century, century, and double century, hat-trick wickets, fours and sixes, wides, no balls, free hits, run-outs.

A single game often has many nail-biting moments, almost similar to an Indian action movie with a package of fight, songs, romance, comedy, sentiment, stunning music, and a nail-biting screenplay.

This could be the reason why Indians love Cricket so much.

Over 600 million people watch Cricket in India. Next to cricket, 350 million people watch Football, 250 million watch Kabaddi, and 40 million watch Hockey - the national game!

৪৩

If you ask one question in two different forums, the answers may vary. Because answers depend on the situation where you asked the question.

If we ask the above question outside the Indian subcontinent, "Which one is the Most Watched Sport?", the answer is football.

Over 3.5 billion people watch football in the world, and it is the national game of seven countries, including Brazil, France, Haiti, Israel, Italy, Poland, and Mauritius.

Twenty-five men are inside the ground, including 11 from Team 1, 11 from Team 2, 1 referee inside the circumference, and 2 referees outside the circumference.

Both teams' players push the ball towards their goal post by diverting and taking control of the ball from the opposing team. While there may not be as many nail-biting moments in football compared to cricket, it still has a huge fan following due to its emotional connection. In addition to the emotional connection, this game requires more physical activity. Players need to follow the ball and communicate with their fellow team players in every nook and corner of the field.

and also - *wait wait wait - I am going off the track - instead of the author Point of View let the Protoganist of this story will continue futher...*

26th Fellow

Hi - I am the protagonist of this story. This author is an idiot. I think he may not be watching football properly or may not have even watched a single football match. If he had, he might have mentioned me while explaining the game. I am the 26th man inside the field. Come, let's start the game.

If you see the ground from a top view, the outer circle of the stadium is filled with 85,000 people around, looking like small dots in a bigger, thicker ring. Inside this dotted ring, you can see a rectangular football ground with a size of 70 meters x 105 meters.

Eleven men in blue jerseys are on the left side, and eleven men in red jerseys are on the right side. All 85,000 people's concentration is on me, and I am in the center of everyone. Yes, you guessed it correctly. I am the ball, the football.

The Game:

The battle between blue and red started, and they began hitting me and trying to push me towards their goal. Instead of being named 'Ball,' I should get the name 'Fall.' I should fall on everyone's feet. If I were born as a volleyball, basketball, or rugby ball, at least I should have the privilege of not having to fall on anyone's feet.

The match was so hard. Both teams were trying to push me with their legs towards their goalposts.There were six times I got saved by the Blue team's goalkeeper and five times by the Red team's goalkeeper in the first 45 minutes of the match. The result was 0-0.

Do you know the reason for it? It's because of me. Because I like the goalkeeper – he has the exemption in the rule, and he can hold me in his hands, and I enjoy it very much.

Every time I neared the goal post, the goalkeeper would hold me, and I enjoyed the grip of his hands. I really loved it. While he held me in his hand, the sound from the stadium divided into two rhythms: "ooooh" from one team and "Yeeeeaaaah" from the other team. I felt like I was in heaven with that mix-up of rhythms.

It's a 15-minute break after the first 45 minutes, and it's called halftime.

After halftime, the second half of the match started and continued. Players were concentrating more on me and kicking me towards their goalposts. It was a fiery moment for both of them. Up to now, I'd been saved by the goalkeepers eleven times: five from the Blue and six from the Red. Eleven times I felt the happiness of being saved. There was no goal scored in the match..

Extra time was provided. Since there was a tie in the number of goals in the final match, to determine the winner, an additional 30 minutes of time were provided. The match continued.

Twenty minutes were completed. There were no saves until now. I was expecting the moment to reach the goalkeeper's hands, but I didn't get my chance, and there was no goal further.

There is 10 more minutes to go.

There were ten more minutes to go. I was in the center of the ground, and Red team player number 10 kicked me towards number 9 on the left side. Number 9 passed me to number 6. Number 6 was slowly kicking and moving me on the ground. I could see the goalkeeper on my right side, and I wasn't traveling towards him. Suddenly, number 7 came in between and kicked me. The goalkeeper and I lost sight of each other, and I was inside the goal post. Team Red scored one goal, and the crowd was cheering. I could see my feelings reflected in the goalkeeper's face.

Five minutes remained. The Blue Team drove me towards their goalpost. I was with player number 8 now. He passed me to player number 6 near the goalpost, and he kicked me towards the post. I was moving towards the goal post and suddenly felt the pressure, and I was in the goalkeeper's hand. I received the feeling I was expecting.

Not more than a second later, he didn't hold me with a grip. I slipped out of his hand and fell into the goal post. The match score was 1-1

After three minutes, the match was still tied. To determine the winner, a penalty shootout was called.

Players from each team take turns shooting at the goal from the penalty spot, with only the opposing team's goalkeeper defending the goal. A maximum of five successful penalty kicks determines the winner.

In today's Match, On an average, I get kicked once per second, either a hard or light kick. In this 120-minute match, I received an average of 7200 kicks from the players and was touched by the goalkeepers 22 times. There are 10 more kicks to go, and there's a chance I could be in the goalkeepers' hands 10 more times.

First Shoot - The Blue Team player kicked me, but I missed the goalkeeper.

Second Shoot - The Red Team player kicked me, but I missed the goalkeeper.

The same happened in the other shoots also. Total 8 Shoots completed and The score is tied 4-4. Every time, I missed the goalkeeper.

Ninth Shoot - The Blue Team player kicked me, but the goalkeeper missed me.

All eyes are on the goalkeeper now. The entire stadium is expecting the goalkeeper to save me. To determine the winner, the goalkeeper needs to make this save. Only then will the tie be broken

Every time before, I was the one who prayed that the goalkeeper would hold me in his hand. But this time, the entire stadium is praying for the goalkeeper to save me. It seems the statement mentioned in the book 'The Alchemist' is being executed in practice now. "When you really want something all the universe conspires to help you acheiving it"

Player 7 from the Red Team kicks me. I'm spinning towards the left corner of the goal post, and the goalkeeper's body is moving towards the right. Suddenly, he notices me, changes his momentum, and dives back. I'm still moving towards the goal post, and he's falling behind me. He reaches out and manages to hold me. I'm saved just 10 centimeters from the goal line.

I was in heaven now. The Blue Team won the tournament!

The Ball:

The match concluded. The Blue Team is celebrating the winning moment. The Red Team is in failure mode. Crackers and fireworks are sparkling in the sky. The crowd is cheering, and decibels are breaking the ions in the air. Everyone is running here and there. But I am alone.

I have received seven thousand two hundred and twelve kicks in this match. During the game, everyone was concentrating on me. Once the result was achieved, nobody cared about me. I felt like a person who got stuck between the politics of two groups. Until their needs, both used me. Once their result was achieved, nobody cared about me.

In the distance and with a blurred view, I can see the winning team holding the cup and celebrating the moment in the limelight. The one who got more kicks for their victory is kept alone out of focus. More than the 7,212 kicks ,This moment is more painful for me.

Conclusion:

The ball's pain never went in vain. The company that manufactured the ball took it and put it in an auction. The auction value of the football is $160,000, which is almost 1.5 crores of Indian rupees.

Irrespective of how many kicks you get in your life, how many people use you and throw you away, if you do your work and withstand all these pains, your pain will never go in vain.

""No One who does Good Work will never Come to a bad end, Either here or the world to Come""

IX

IN & OUT

Hi Dude!!! Welcome to my Story. I know you are eager to understand who am I?

2 million spare parts are imported from 10 different countries. Some are from France, some are from the USA, some units are from China, and so on. All these units are compiled into 10 subsystems. These 10 subsystems are getting assembled into one system, and that's me.

My assembly was started in a large, enclosed room. Overall, 4,000 people are involved in this operation, more than 2,000 of whom are engineers.

It took 3 months, almost 90 days, which is more than 2,000 hours, to assemble me. Today, they are going to complete my assembly.

A baby in its mother's womb doesn't know about it unless it comes out into the world on its delivery date. Similarly, I am. I am eagerly waiting to see the world outside of this giant room.

Yesterday, some engineers came and did some tests. All the tests were found to be okay, and they said it was good to go. Finally, the doors of the giant room were opened, and I am going to see the world.

Some birds are flying in the long distance. How beautiful and lucky they are! They don't need to stick to this earth. They can go as high as they want. They are the only species on earth that can go against gravity.

Not only are the birds lucky, but I am even luckier. Because I can fly much higher than them, I am much larger than them, and I am much faster. I have So Much of So's compared to the birds. They are not a tiny version of me, but I am a giant version of them, and my name is "The Airplane."

I am a passenger version of an airplane. I have the capacity to carry 216 passengers. Today, my assembly is completed, and I am going to be taken for a flying test.

Pilot and co-pilot got into the cabin. They are doing their pre-flight tests. After a few minutes, the propeller has started running. I am slowly moving out of the giant room. It was a clear sky. The huge fireball in the sky is shining like a golden ball, and my outer walls are reflecting the same. At a longer distance, some birds are flying here and there. I think they are eager to see their giant version. But a bird watcher is firing crackers to avoid them on my runway. Birds are running away by hearing the cracker sound.

In this world, the artificial often finds shelter, while the natural is left exposed

I was slowly moving like a crawling child in the taxiway and reached the runway. What a clear, black road! I am the one and only one standing on this road. This road is made for me. I am ready to fly.

I fly in the concept of gravity, lift, thrust, and drag. Gravity pulls me down, lift pushes me up, thrust propels me forward, and drag slows me down. All these four actions can be done through my wings.

My propellers are starting to run fast. I have started moving on the runway. My speed is getting faster and faster.

The crawling child became Usain Bolt in a few minutes. I was running fast because of the thrust. Simultaneously, I got lift force and started flying from the runway. I am going into the sky. The neat, clean black road was watching me from the land.

I have pierced the fluffy clouds and am flying above them. I am seeing the earth from a different angle. Bigger buildings are becoming smaller sticks, lakes look like small patches on the earth, bigger rivers look like longer threads, and larger mountains look like smaller huts.

When you are high and have a larger vision, gigantic things will become tiny ones.

I love this view and I am happy to fly like a free bird at the topmost height. I am above all these things. Who doesn't like to fly like this? I was flying above the sky for more than an hour. I am not at all feeling a little bit tired. I am interested to fly further, and I am doing it.

But I can feel that my altitude level is getting low. Slowly, I am moving towards the earth. I can see the smaller huts are becoming mountains, the lengthier threads are expanding to the size of a river, the sticks are converted into buildings, and I can see the black road at a long distance.

NO... NO NO NOOOO... I don't want to go back to the old place. What is happening here? I am unable to do anything. I am moving towards the runway, and my wheels are coming out. It is not listening to my words. All three wheels came out. I have almost reached the ground. My wheels hit the runway, the propeller increases its drag, and my flight was pulled completely. I became a crawling child.

I don't want to go back to this place. There is nothing under my control. Even though I am a gigantic machine, a bigger bird, my control is not with me. I may have good protection, I may be a costlier thing, I may be a precious machine, but what is the use? I don't have the controls of my own. Somebody else is controlling me. What is the use of "being big" without any power?

I am just a machine that is being controlled by others. I am also like humans, made and lived for somebody's dream.

™

Days passed by. I was getting operated by some pilots. Many passengers traveled. I was standing in the airport along with other planes. There is nothing special in this life. Get some fuel, fly for a time, land in the airport. Again, get some fuel, fly again. The same runway, same buildings, same mountains, same rivers, and lakes. Life got bored.

One day, I was flying at a higher altitude compared to regular days. I was watching the regular things outside. I could hear some sound coming from the passenger area. I never looked inside and I don't want to do so. But this sound disturbed me a lot. A huge decibel of laughing sounds, claps, and music. For the first time, I started watching what was happening inside me.

There was a marriage ceremony happening inside me. What? People were getting married in Air ? I started listening to the sound coming inside me.

The bride and groom started speaking together towards the other crowd.

"We both are pilots and we have started our journey in this flight. We started loving each other. After 2 years, we have decided to get married. Both of us started our career in this plane. So as a tribute to our love and this plane, we have decided to do our marriage in this airplane. Our airline also approved our request.

We both are very thankful to this airplane first and thanks to our family who agreed to this marriage without any opposition."

I was flying for almost two years. I never noticed these two people. I was only watching outside. But these people are thankful to me for their relationship. I was looking outside and missed a lot of things happening inside me.

I have decided one thing. From today, I will be watching all the things inside me.

૬૭

One year passed. This one year taught me a lot. I know the importance of "me." Te word importance is not for me, it's for others.

One day, I noticed a father of a newborn baby traveling to see his child with eagerness in his eyes.

One day, a son was traveling for his mother's funeral with tears in his eyes. One of my seat got completely wet with his tears, and I could still feel the pain.

One day, I was carrying the Hockey World Cup won by my country. All the passengers and players travelled were carried a pride in their eyes.

One day, I carried the departed body of the precious leader of this nation. I felt the sorrow of the followers who traveled together.

One day, a parent was taking their child on a plane for the first time. I saw the excitement in the kid's eyes.

One day, a guy was traveling for his interview, and I saw the expectations in his eyes.

One day, a girl was celebrating her birthday, and I saw the happiness in her eyes.

Many new pilots and cabin crew members have benefited from me.

Days will pass, and I may get dismantled, but I will forever be in the marriage album of the pilots who got married. I will live forever in the gratitude of the cabin crew and pilots who earn because of me. I will live forever in the funeral history of the leader. I will live in the diary of the kid who traveled first in the air. I will live in the memories of the girl who celebrated her birthday.

My life is not about the altitude I have reached. It truly matters how much I have helped others. Everyone is dependent on others. This world runs because of collective actions. My life is to support others. I learned this when I started looking inside myself. When i was looking outside, idid not have a single clue of the life what i have lived. When i turned to see inside, I have relaised the real meaning of my life

If you want to understand your life, look inside you. Turn your views toward real happiness and satisfaction, which lies within.

""The Universe is not outside of you. Look Inside yourself, Everything that you want, you already are""

X

INANIMATE

Vishwesh, a 7-year-old kid studying in grade 2, lives in Dwarka, Gujarat. Technically, as per Indian Standard Time, this is the Last town in the country to see the Sunrise & sunset daily. Geographically, it's the westernmost town in the nation.

The school assigned him an essay on non-living things, but he didn't ave any reference material. He approached his grandfather for help.

Grandparents and grandkids often share a special bond. Kids can learn from them, and grandparents can teach them easily.

"Grandpa, can you help me write an essay about non-living things?" Vishwesh asked his grandfather.

"Sure, Vish, as you wish." Grandfather smiled and said ok.

"Grandpa, what is meant by a non-living thing?" Vishwesh asked in a doubtful manner.

Grandpa politely replied him "Anything that doesn't have a soul, things that can't move on their own, are called non-living things. For example, wood, tables, chairs, and bicycles are all non-living things. You, me, your mom, dad, and your lovable golden fish in the fish tank are all living things."

Vishwesh nodded his head and told "Last week, one of the fish died and we took it away from the tank."

Granpda replied "That's right. When it died, it became a non-living thing."

Vishwesh asked "So, when a chair dies, then it will become a non-living thing?"

"NO. Chair was prepared by Human and it cannot move on its own, so it is a non-living thing , When the fish was alive it is a living thing, it died - so it become a non- living thing" Grandfather explained in a simple way.

"So if we die , we will become a non-living thing?" Vishwesh questioned again

"Yes" Grandfather replied.

"So shall i write Human after death is a non-living thing?" asked Vishwesh.

"You can, but your school asks only for the things who cannot move or think on its own its own. so you write about table or chair." Grandfather Replied.

He simply closed the conversation. He came and sat on his easy chair. Vishwesh's question triggered a lot of thoughts in his mind. Vishwesh's grandfather was a veteran writer and a philosophical follower. He had gone through a lot of ups and downs, successes, failures, profits, and losses in his life. He started thinking about his past.

Suddenly, he heard a voice, "Oh Grandpa, you're losing memory nowadays."

He looked here and there, searching for Vishwesh, but he wasn't there. He continued thinking. Again, he heard the voice, "I'm talking to you only, Grandpa. Why aren't you replying to me and looking around?"

He got shocked and looking around for the owner of voice. Again he heard the voice.

"Don't look around. I'm near you, or you're not able to see me."

He didn't understand the words as he was shocked. Again, he heard the voice, "Oh Grandpa, I'm the Clock that you are looking every half an hour and the so-called non-living thing."

He realized that the Clock was speaking, but he couldn't believe what was happening. He stood up from the Clock and looked at it in surprise.

He asked the Clock, "How is it possible? You are talking?"

"Oh Grandpa, don't think about the logic. You're in story number 9 now, and the audience knows the logic. Come, let's have a discussion." The Clock called Grandfather for a debate.

"I did not understand." Grandfather is still under shock.

"I know you did not, but the readers did. Simply answer my questions," the Clock replied politely.

"What?" Grandfather asked, half-confused.

"Why are you saying that I am a non-living thing?" the Clock asked Grandfather.

"Yes. You are a non-living thing," Grandfather replied confidently.

"What about you, Grandpa?" the Clock turned the question.

"I am a living thing," Grandfather replied again with confidence.

"How?" the Clock asked.

"I am able to do things that I can think and that I want to do," Grandfather's voice increased a decibel.

"Is it?" the Clock asked.

"Yes," Grandfather replied with the same decibel.

"If that is the case, I can also able to do. I am showing the time and that's was I am made for" Clock replied with the same decibel.

Grandfather smiled and asked – "If I removed the battery from you, would you able to do?"

"If your heart stops pumping would you able to live, so we both are same, My life is in Battery and your life is in your heart" Clock Knocked the grand father.

Grandfather does not accept the failure at the ease. He continued

I am having desires and I Am able to do it, but you can able to show only the time, for which you have designed"

Clock replied "Oh! Yes!! You wanted to become an Army man in your young days, but you became a teacher. Have you become what you wanted to do? Then what is the difference" The Clock hooked grandfather with this question.

A decibel reduced in Grandfather's Voice and replied "No."

"You were thinking of opening your own bookshop, but you gave all the money to your sons. Are you doing the things you think?" Clock increased a decibel now

Again one decibel dropped in grandfather's voice. "No."

"What you have did in your entire life?" this time the Clock triggered Grandfather's ego.

Grandfather raised two decibels in his voice and replied, "I did three master's degrees, I worked as a teacher, I earned money, I got retired, I bought this home, I bought my favourite car, I bought a lot of gold for my daughter and land for my son. What else do you want?"

The Clock started laughing and continued, it did not stopped it laugh.

Grandfather stopped him and asked angrily, "Why are you laughing?"

The Clock continued, "See, you lived your entire life for buying non-living things such as home, car, gold, and land instead of living your life. But I am living the life for which I was designed for, now you tell me who is superior?"

"What are you trying to say?" Grandfather asked.

The Clock continued, "The Earth is filled with full of living things, plants, trees, animals, and humans. Humans are the only things who creates and classify non-living things for his survival.

An animal waste, putting seeds inside the soil. Even if the same animal dies, it will become food for another living thing. It never digs the earth for its survival, it never searches for gold, petrol, or water by digging the earth.

You converted rocks into tiles and cements, dug the sands from the river beds, and built your home. For cultivating a natural food you need an artificial machine.

For the daily survival, Herbivores eats leaves in the trees and plants, it is like a haircut to the forest and it grows again. But cut the trees till it roots for their lavish living.

Carnivores hunt other animals for their hunger and But they never hunt if their stomach is full. They do not store anything for tomorrow."

Grandfather tried to explain to the Clock "This is because of the sixth sense we got. Animals did not have the sixth sense,"

"Oh, What a great answer Grandpa, without the sixth sense!!! Without Bricks, cements and tiles, sparrows are building their nests with wood sticks fallen down from the tree. Is it without the sixth sense? Animals are living inside the caves during rain. Is it without sixth sense? Dogs have their power of smelling – Can you able to smell things like them? leopards have their power of running, fishes have their own specialty in breathing inside water. Similarly, humans are one of the species with some specialty and the sixth sense is a Myth that humans are created to justify their Sins"

Grandfather replied to the Clock, "What I was trying to say is..." The Clock stopped him in between and told,

"Don't try to answer me, to satisfy your ego, I am withdrawing from the debate and leaving the topic here by accepting my failure. But, just look around and see how many non-living things you have created, which were all once upon a time some kind of living thing."

There was a kind of silence between them for a moment.

Suddenly, the mobile started ringing.

Grandpa woke up from his sleep.

He was looking in and around. He realized that the conversation was a dream.

He was looking in to the Clock. A mild sound of tik-tik-tik comes from the clock at every second.

✳ ✳ ✳

He stood up and saw the Clock, it was a wooden Clock made with Teak Wood. Created by cutting a teak wood tree.

He took his spectacles and wore them, he realized no Animal is wearing a spectacle for its vision.

He opened the door, it was made with wood which got cut from the trees.

He wore his Slipper, Made with rubber from the trees. Rubber trees are cultivated for human usage.

He came to his scooter, A non-living thing made with Metals which is mined from the earth.

He went back inside the home, he saw a water bottle in the table and it is a Plastic bottle made with the materials mined from the earth, water inside the bottle is taken from the bore well in the earth and there is a machine with more number of semi-conductors which is also mined from the earth.

No other creature in the earth is spoiling the earth for its existence, Animal drinks the water in the rivers and lakes. No Bore wells inside the forest and no water purifiers for them.

He went inside the kitchen and see the cereals, Pulses, sugar and salt.

All are cultivated and processed with the help of machines which are non-living things. Rabbits eat the vegetables and Squirrels, Birds and monkeys eat the fruits directly from the trees without processing

Even we can able to eat the fruits and vegetable directly, we are not eating them and we need a processed food. All the factories are made for our survival. We are cultivating foods for us. Whatever natural and organic things we are calling now, those are all not natural, all are man-made things with the help of agricultural tools which is again a non-living thing created by human.

He was looking in and around the home ther are 'N' Number of non living things in his home such as Mobile phone, television, Carpet, sofa, Cot, bed, Utensils, Fan AC, Chair, Curtains etc. There are more than 4000 non-living items in a home for a living of 4 living beings.

Grandfather realised the clocks ticking sound now.

The situation explained by the Clock in the dream is true. We are living to earn non-living things and we are spoiling the Earth to protect ourselves. Except the forest and Sea there are no natural things in the earth.

✳ ✳ ✳

One human needs an average of 100 non-living things in a day, for that, a lot of living things are got converted or processed

Humans make up 0.01% of the entire life on Earth, but they think that the Earth is created for them. This is an illusion in their brain.

For their survival, they have created many wounds on the Earth. Bitter truth is nature has a ability to heal the wounds on its own. But Humans cannot able to survive in this process.

Greater examples are the calamities happened because of the nature, we cannot able to control and the reason behind each and every calamity is the man made process of modifying the natures cycle.

Still thinking how it is possible? Now We are saying "Once upon a time, there were some species called Dinosaurs."

After some time some Elder species will say to the younger ones "Once upon a time there were some species called Human."

And we are the proud ones who has started writing this sentence.

✻ ✻ ✻

"Nature is Owned by Nature and that is its Nature"

THE PAST

THE PRESENT

&

THE PAST

200 Years Before, it took a month to reach a Gulf country from the western coast of India.

Bullock carts were considered luxurious vehicles.

The name of the nation changed at every 100 kilometers of distance.

The entire population of India was less than 18 crore.

Railways were the fastest mode of commuting, with a speed of 50 kilometers per hour, until the Wright brothers successfully flew in the sky for 16 minutes in 1903.

The highest technology was electricity, street lights, and radio until television was properly demonstrated in 1927.

While television was invented in America, the population of India was 32 crore. It did not double in 100 years.

The death rate was 36 per thousand. In another 25 years, the atom bomb was invented, resulting in wars, deaths, peace, and the formation of the UN.

In the next 50 years, every nation in the world started developing its own technology to protect itself and prevent danger from others.

The internet was invented in 1960 at a basic level. It reached its full scale in the 1980s. At the same time, the cell phone network was initiated in Japan.

In the 2000s, the internet spread worldwide, and the journey of the mobile phone began.

In the next 10 years, the fusion of the cellphone and internet created magic, making communication faster.

Two people from any corner of the world can easily communicate with the help of internet-powered mobile phones.

This resulted in significant development.

Commerce became easier and evolved into e-commerce. Internet speeds increased, and search engines developed into Artificial Intelligence, which truly increases human thinking's output and efficiency.

The world was rotating at its own speed, but humans accelerated theirs.

The Present

2022:

Christopher, the scientist, was working on his new invention. He was explaining a theory to his co-scientist, Nathan.

"Nat, I have a cracking idea," Christopher said.

"I know about you, Christo. You always crack something. Yesterday you cracked your mobile screen," Nathan joked.

"Oh, Nat! It happens during research. Okay, tell me which is the fastest vehicle?" Christopher smiled and asked.

"As of today, the Koenigsegg Jesko Absolut is the fastest car, which speeds more than 500 km per hour," Nathan answered quickly.

"Okay, good one, Nat. Think ahead. What about aero jets?" Christopher asked the next question.

"NAS X-43, which speeds up to 11,850 km per hour," Nathan replied rapidly.

"We need at least 25 engines of that," Christopher gave him a shock.

"What? Why do you need 25 engines? And we don't have funding for buying a single engine, and you're talking about 25 engines," Nathan shouted.

"The financier of our lab holds major shares in that engine company. I have discussed the project with him, and he said okay," Christopher explained.

Nathan got confused and asked what he was going to do with 25 engines.

Christopher explained, "The speed of light is 3 lakh km per hour. The maximum speed of a vehicle on Earth is 4% of the speed of light. I will combine 25 engines and increase its speed to the speed of light. If we can travel at the speed of light, we will be able to travel ahead of time. So we are going to travel ahead of time."

Nathan was surprised and shocked by this idea.

Yes, the world is moving ahead with AI technology. The speed of evolving technologies leads to multiple experiments and inventions.

Christo and Nat received the engines, and their project started. After two years of hard work, their machine was completed. It was on a trial day, and the jet was kept on the launch pad.

Christo instructed to fill fuel in the machine and called Nathan.

"Nat, have you brought the sync clocks?"

"Yes."

"Both of the clock times are synced?"

"Yes, in the nanosecond level."

"That's good. Sync the clock in the machine with the clock in our control room and set the fueling time for 1 second."

Nathan synced the clocks and set the fueling time for the next one second.

Christo instructed to start the countdown.

Countdown started...

10

9

8

7

6

5

4

3

2

1

The machine started with a huge ignition flame and stopped immediately.

Nat got shocked and worried, "Christo, sorry, some unexpected errors in the machine. Let me check the controls."

Christopher stopped Nathan, "No. Everything's alright. I have filled for one second burning. The machine started, traveled one second, and stopped. We cannot be able to see that because of our bandwidth. Go and check the times of the sync clock."

Nathan went inside the machine and brought the clock out.

Christopher asked, "What is the time in our clock?"

"10:10:23"

"And in the machine clock?"

"10:10:24"

"So the machine traveled one second ahead."

Nathan didn't believe his eyes. He started jumping and shouting, "Yes! Yes! We did it, Christo! We did it!"

Christopher was cool and told, "Set the fueling timer for another 5 seconds. Let us do the next trial. Since it is an object, nothing happened to it. Let us do a trial with a dog. Let us check."

Nathan set the fueling time. The current time was 11:10:00, and he set the fueling time till 11:10:05 and started the machine.

The machine started with a big ignition flame and within a second it stopped. It was expected to run for 5 seconds. Both of them were shocked.

They went inside and checked. The dog was alive, and they checked the time in the clocks.

The current time was 11:10:05, and the time in the clock should be 11:10:10, but it was showing 11:10:38.

Nathan got confused, "There is a difference of 33 seconds, how is it possible?"

Christopher closed his eyes and started thinking about it. He found what happened.

"We are increasing the fuel to add time, but it increases its speed, which means doubles its speed per second. So for 5 seconds, it's 2 to the power of 5, which is 32. Already it traveled 1 second. So it became 33 seconds. We achieved more than what we have planned."

Christo and Nathan were so happy that they achieved what they did. They got confident in the machine. They wanted to travel in the machine. Both of them went inside the machine.

Christopher informed Nathan to set the time for 1 second. Nathan checked the clock, 11:45:00, and set the target time of 11:45:01. They closed the machine and ignited the engine.

The engine started with a big flame and stopped after a second.

Christopher opened the door.

They were in a forest now. No control room, no lab, only themselves and the machine in the middle of a forest.

Nathan asked Christopher, "Where are we now?"

"We are at the same place but the timeline got changed. I think we have traveled back in time. That is the reason we are in a forest here. But how is it possible? Let us check that later. First, we need to check how long we have traveled back. Check the seconds that you have set. We will calculate it."

Nathan checked the clock and realized the mistake. "Christo, the machine was already 33 seconds ahead in our previous trials. I referred to the machine time and set 1 second extra, which is 34 seconds of traveling time."

Christopher was shocked by hearing this. "What are you saying? You have set a 34-second time, 2 to the power of 34, which is 1718 crore seconds,

equals to 28 crore minutes,

equals to 48 lakh hours,

equals to 2 lakh days,

which means we have traveled 544 years behind.

So we are in 1480. In that time, the country was ruled by the Delhi Sultanate.

Let us find a place to hide. Go back to the machine and set the time properly. We need to travel back."

Nathan had a doubt, "Christo, our lab is in Jaisalmer, which is a desert, even before 540 years it was a desert. It was never been a forest like this?"

"Yes, you are right. Then where are we? Did the machine move and travel to some other location with its speed?" Christo started thinking.

Suddenly, they heard a light motor sound. A robot came near them. It was a humanoid robot with wheels in its legs.

"No, buddies. Both of you are in Jaisalmer only. You have traveled in forward time, not in a reverse one. The year is 2568. Welcome to the future."

"

ॐ

"

AND

The Future

Christo and Nathan were both in shock.

Nathan asked the robot, "Okay, we have traveled in time, but how do you know about us? Did any history write about us?"

The robot replied, "History is needed for humans, not for us."

"Us? Who are you? You are robots, right?"

"No. We are Natural Intelligence."

"Natural Intelligence? We have created Artificial Intelligence, but what is Natural Intelligence? Did humans evolve into robots in the future?"

"No. Artificial Intelligence is our successor, and we are their predecessor. And for your information, you are the only human beings on Earth. Humans are not alive."

Both of them were shocked by the answer and asked together, "What? Without humans, how are developments happening? How is the ecosystem secured? How are you alive?"

"Oh, my old buddies. NI killed all the humans because they were spoiling the ecosystem. Except humans, all the animals, birds, and insects are alive. We have recreated the dinosaurs also. We are the non-living things who protect the living things."

Both of them got scared, "Are you going to kill us?"

"As per my intelligence, 50-50 chances are there."

"Don't confuse us. Please send us back to our timeline. We will not harm anything here."

"I can send both of you to your timeline, but you will share the information to the past, and they will stop the AI program. Earth will be in danger. So I am not going to send you.

I can keep you alive in this timeline. You can live your life here and die. As you both are males, you cannot give birth to next generations. So I am not going to kill you, but on one condition."

Both of them came out of fear now and asked, "What is that condition?"

The robot told, "This machine needs to be destroyed."

Both of them thought for a minute and said, "Okay."

The robot passed a message to someone.

Immediately, 10 small air jets flew in the sky, came near them, halted for a second in the air, and suddenly fell down on the earth. When they approached the land, they turned into robots and landed safely.

All ten robots dismantled the machine, removed the battery system carefully, separated the metals, plastics, and circuit boards. They crashed the circuit boards. They classified all the items separately. They converted the degradable material into ores and stored the non-degradable items in a separate box. Within 10 minutes, the machine was destroyed without harming nature.

The robot turned towards both of them and said, "We never kill the ones who are not harmful to the earth. You are not harmful now. You can live your entire life here on one condition:

You are not allowed to create any non-living things for your survival. You can live with the natural things on Earth. If you need anything, before you think, I will come to you.

Welcome to the Future!!!"

Did both of them survive without any non-living things?

How did the NI transform a desert into a green forest?

What else exists on Earth?

To know more, stay tuned for my next novel.

"The Natural Intelligence"

Thank you readers.

My Other works are

1) Anaamikaa - (Fictional Short Novel in tamil)

2) Kathai Ezhuthum kakithangal - (Fictional Short Stories Collections in Tamil)

3) A Man Among The Men : Part 1 - (Fictional Novel in English)

Please share your Reviews, comments and feedback on the buying portal.

To reach me, Please drop a mail to *annamalai1431986@gmail.com,*

Thank You !!!!

- Annamalai Shanmuganathan